The Road to Whatever;

A Pop Culture Approach to Buddhism

By: cara rios

"Just as, a dark lotus or a white lotus, born in the water, comes to full growth in the water, rises to the surface and stands unspotted by the water, even so, the Buddha, having come to full growth in the world, passing beyond the world, abides unspotted by the world." (Sumyutta Nikaya 22.94)

iUniverse, Inc.
New York   Bloomington

The Road to Whatever
a pop culture approach to Buddhism

iUniverse books may be ordered through booksellers or by contacting:

iUniverse
1663 Liberty Drive
Bloomington, IN 47403
www.iuniverse.com
1-800-Authors (1-800-288-4677)

ISBN: 978-1-4401-2162-3 (pbk)
ISBN: 978-1-4401-2163-0 (ebk)

Printed in the United States of America

iUniverse rev. date: 1/26/2009

I dedicate this book with my deepest love and gratitude to Mia and Maya Carrillo who are my favorite teachers, my best students, my dearest friends, my little sisters; my daughters!

Table of Contents

Introduction:

I discovered Buddhism in my early 30's at a time of my life in which I was searching for spiritual enlightenment to manage the day in and day out factors of life; dating, working, family, all the stuff we all struggle with on a daily basis. Two years ago I would not have imagined that today I would be writing a book about spiritual enlightenment, let alone Buddhism. When I found the eightfold path I immersed myself into the study and practice of these philosophies. The more I practiced the more I began to see many aspects of my life change from extreme to moderate; as I felt my way through this new found knowledge I felt like a blind mouse running through a labyrinth. At first finding my way through it was all hit, misses and hard knocks along the way until I began to gain a sensation of awakening; slowly I began to find peace and serenity in my life.

Because of my discovery of Buddhism and the eightfold path I now better understood certain facts of life and I have learned to accept circumstances that beyond my control. I slowly began to train myself to be still and to understood that there are situations and circumstances in life that can not be changed, like the fact that there are cruel, ugly people in this world, and that I may not be able to change how they behave, however, I am able to change how I will allow their ugly actions to affect me. I also cannot control which one of my girlfriends will finding her Prince Charming next; and when she'll get the big rock, but I can change whether or not I will feel genuinely happy for them or if I will just fake my support when truly I feel a vague indifference towards their happiness.

One of the greatest things that I have discovered about Buddhism is that we can choose to show compassion towards all living things, to live joyously, jubilantly or we can choose to do exact opposite and to live in an endless cycle of suffering. Which ever we choose… "WE CHOOSE".

One of the downfalls about finding the road to enlightenment is that the more that I learned, the more I realized that our contemporary value system and the standards by which we gage success, happiness and righteous living are distorted and out of sync with nature. In nature every entity from the smallest to the largest has a purpose, for the most part a single purpose. If it is an ant then its purpose is to work for the good of the unit. A cat's purpose is to chase mice. A fruit tree's purpose is to produces a specific fruit and so on, but not us humans we somehow managed to evade a natural order and a specific purpose, we as Cart man of South Park says "We do what we want" and we want it all. We want to do and to have everything both tangible and intangible; whether it is to fly all over the world, to speed in fancy cars, becoming YouTube superstars, or being MySpace Don Juans & Divas, we just want it all and the more things we can get or do the better people we believe ourselves to be.

However, the idea that the more that we have the greater we are is the very conflict of our nature and our purpose, because wanting and desiring more only imprisons us deeper into our cycle of suffering and longing. I once heard a Buddhist fable about a greedy young prince; I think this story captures our society's hunger and greed for more fairly accurately. We, similar to the young prince in this fable, find ourselves wanting everything we see, we want lots of it and we want it fast. If you are like me and most other people you've probably tried a ton of different activities trying to find yourself, however the key is not in finding oneself in activities but finding activities that we love. It simply cannot work the other way around or else we'll spend all our time and energy jumping around from one thing to another and never fulfill our desire for happiness. Let's see if the adventure of the young prince in the story hit a cord?

There was once a young prince, who had almost everything his heart desired, but he wanted more. One day the prince kills his father and becomes the king. He becomes the most powerful man, and people fear him. When he passes everyone bows down to him.

One day he notices that the sun is shining in his eye. He says "bow down, sun", but the sun would not bow. So he decides that he will become the sun and become even more powerful than any king. So he becomes the sun in the sky and blazes down on everything and everyone. He's content for awhile.

Then one day clouds fill the sky and it rains for days. The sun says to the clouds "get out of my path you clouds", but the clouds do not listen and they continue to block the sun's path. This makes the sun so angry that he decides that he will become the clouds and cover the sun whenever he feels like it and he will make it rain down whenever he wants. So he becomes the clouds in the sky. He makes it rain for days un-end. And once again he is content.

A few days pass and then some very strong winds blow in; the wind blows the clouds right out of the sky. When the prince sees this he decides right then and there that the wind is far more powerful than the sun or the clouds or any king or anything else he could think of so he decides right then and there to become the wind. So he becomes the wind. He begins blowing here and there; uprooting whatever he feels like uprooting. He goes around starting tornados and causing chaos. And once again he is content.

One day in the middle of his chaos he notices that the rocks on the ground don't move when he blows over them. He goes crazy "why don't they move?" He doesn't get it; he figures that a single rock must be more powerful yet than any of the things he has been thus far, so he immediately turns himself into a rock.

Finally, all he can do is lay there in the ground. He cannot move or cause chaos and he is not feared by anyone and he has no power. He's just a rock that lies in the ground. And the young prince is content, but not really.

One day a boy comes by and begins to play a game just kicking the rock around, laughing and having fun just kicking the rock. The boy is happy, he really is.

The prince decides then that what he wants to be more than anything is what he was a happy boy kicking a rock around just as he was in the beginning. He just wants to be a boy, but this time he can't do anything about it, because now he's just a rock lying in the dirt.

Sounds familiar? We are just like the young prince in the story, find ourselves constantly chasing one thing and then another seeking out new adventures, trying to reach new heights of power and wanting to feel new experiences. Most of the time only to end up completely disappointed with our choices. To a certain degree that's what life is all about, but the danger comes with the extremes. When we take it too far it becomes a cycle of suffering, for instance a married man or woman that likes having the security of marriage, but wants to have more adventure in his or her life so he or she seeks out an extra marital affair, this becomes suffering for all involved. Other examples might be a student that constantly switches focus going from one discipline to another only to never finish any given discipline. Just like the prince in the story we find satisfaction in what we chase but once we have it the satisfaction it gives us has a very short lifespan. In fact it seems that we are never truly satisfied or grateful for what we have and that's what cause an endless cycle of suffering. Often times it seems that we are so tightly wrapped up in getting what we want that we don't live for the moment but rather we live for the "what's next?" and in doing so we don't allow ourselves to ever really enjoy the experience of being alive. Our minds constantly seek more fun, more power, more beautiful things; more of whatever, but whatever that whatever may be it never suffices. Tao Lao said our mind is like a monkey curious and constantly getting in and out of trouble.

In fact as a writer my mind seems to be quite like a monkey's mind because I constantly construct and deconstruct stories, images, ideas, etc, and my mind has caused me a great deal of frustration during my journey to self enlightenment because it constantly finds new things to focus on. Since Buddhism does not spell everything out for us, but requires that we discover life on our own at the beginning of my journey it was frustrating to understand the Buddha's lessons as I found them ambiguous and difficult to apply to my everyday life situations as there are no commandments or scriptures and the philosophies are ambiguous and left to our personal interpretation. Often times I found myself wondering "What does that mean?" But like everything else in life as I became more comfortable with the philosophies, they became clearer and eventually even vaguely familiar. As I began to practice "right mind" the dots began to connect and I had an "aha moment" "I see, this relates to this aspect of life". Then I found that the lessons were not entirely new to me, which makes a lot of sense as Buddhist philosophies are universal meaning that anyone can practice them and they'll have the same effect regardless of status. Buddha himself taught the path to enlighten for forty-five years to men and women, to the rich and the poor without making the slightest distinction among them. It doesn't matter who you are, how old you are, how wealthy or how poor you are, if you practice Buddha's lessons you will find your path to Nirvana. Though the lessons work the same way for everyone, the journey is different for each one of us. Each one of us has to find our own way on the road to whatever. We can only accomplish this by staying true to ourselves and by opening up to love and compassion.

Later as my understanding of Buddhism grew I began to feel hopeful, I found that some of the Buddhist metaphors seemed remarkably similar to others that I have heard the past "But where?" was the big question. And then the light bulb came on, we're not as lost as I originally thought. These stories although not called Buddhism, Zen or Taoism are the same as those we teach in Western culture when story telling, in fables that teach about good vs. evil. Oddly enough I found a link between Buddhist metaphors and Pop Culture flicks, CHICK FLICKS to be exact! I found that the heroines in some

CHICK FLICKS on a journey of self discovery end up on the eightfold path to get where they want or need to be.

It occurred to me that there's something illusive about the notion of "Whatever". Yes the cliché "talk to the hand cause I don't want to hear it", the "eye rolling"; "chicken head" motion of "Whatever" that Generation Y has made notoriously famous for blabbing out in self-defense, when indifferent, and/or when they're just going with the flow. Yes I said "Whatever!"

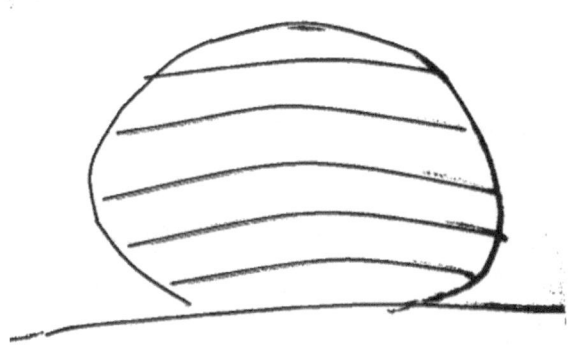

Chapter 1

Simply Whatever

Before we begin exploring the basic Buddhist philosophies, I think it is important to do a brief explanation of the meaning of "Whatever". For our purpose "Whatever" is an affirmative statement, it's an acceptance and a beckoning. Whatever is a concurrence, an agreement of sorts, and not to be confused with not caring. "Whatever" can be as light hearted as just going with the flow "like whatever!" It can also be a declaration to deal with and handle anything that comes accordingly "Whaaat Everrrr!", or it can be kind of the middle of the road "Whatever" either way. Buddhism too is a religion of the middles, in fact the middle road is said to be the path to enlightenment. The middle road is a life of moderation without extremes, which often can be easier said than done, particularly in Western culture because we are constantly being bombarded with stimuli of wanting more, of need more, of wanting bigger and better and being made to feel somewhat inadequate without the newest, biggest, better thing, the hottest chick, the coolest guy, etc....

For the purpose of this book, "Whatever" means nothing and everything; just as Nirvana is a state of nothingness yet all encompassing. "Whatever" can be a very powerful statement that tells you exactly where a person stands on any given matter in one simple word. It can be a summons, perhaps the kind of thing that a nemesis might say to another to beckon or taunt to the other "WHATEVER!"

As I checked my frame of reference of the concept of "Whatever" and according to Merriam-Webster's dictionary, I found a couple of definitions for "Whatever", all of which support the idea that whatever is an affirmative statement.

1. No matter what: *Do it, whatever happens.*
2. Any or any one of a number of things whether specifically known or not: *papers, magazines, or whatever.*
3. Used to indicate indifference to a state of affairs, situation, previous statement, etc.

See "Whatever" in a way is nothingness and everything the same as Nirvana. Nirvana is a state of mind of nothingness and completeness; Nirvana can only be reached by those who become fully awake. So for the sake of this book "Whatever" and Nirvana are one and the same. In other words finding the road to Nirvana is the same as finding the road to Whatever!

Chapter 2

The Four Noble Truths

*"You take the good; you take the bad and there
you have the facts of life, the facts of life"*

Remember Trootie, Natalie, Blaire, Joe and Mrs. Garret? Well, Buddha himself would have given them kudos because taking the good and taking the bad is exactly what he was talking about 2500 years ago, those are the facts of life and they are still true today. Now that we've amply covered the concept of whatever, let's dive into some of the most essential Buddhist philosophies. The first thing to be said about Buddhism is that it is not a religion of beliefs, doctrine or traditions; it is however, a path of growth and liberation. You may ask "Liberation of what?" Well, liberation from everything that imprisons us like worries, anxieties, ambitions, greed, anger, and misguided passion; these emotions are all mental and spiritual prisons that we create for ourselves. We get stuck on the idea that we must to have this or that in order to be happy.

Over twenty-five hundred years ago Prince Siddhartha of India then twenty-nine years old (only 2 years younger than I am now) underwent a series of life changing events that lead to him to an elevated state of mental awareness. Prince Siddhartha reached a level of consciousness that few had managed before him or since him. The once sheltered young prince set out on a journey of self-realization and along the way stumbled upon the keys to the human condition and eternal peace. One night Prince Siddhartha abandoned his palace like a thief in the night while the entire kingdom slept. During his journey Prince Siddhartha, who later came to be known as "Buddha the enlightened one" literally went from riches to rags going from one extreme to the other. The first thing he did when he left his palace was to join a group of Ascetics, which are hermit like people that practice non-violence and respect nature above all else. Some of the rituals and customs of the Ascetics were extremely radical; many were nudist and followed very strict disciplines and vows of poverty which included deprivation and strict meditation. It was during this time that Buddha learned meditation methods and trained his body to endure extremely harsh conditions and deprivations. He eventually came to the conclusion that the road to spiritual enlightenment is the middle road, no extremes. Hence, the reason that Buddhism is now known as a religion of middles.

Since its inception twenty-five hundred years ago Buddhism has undergone a multitude of cultural adaptations based on the countries that the religion has spread to. For instance in China there is Taoism which is the form of Buddhism primarily practiced there, where as in Japan there is Zen Buddhism, which has become the most popular form of Buddhism practiced there. Across the board however, whether Zen, Taoism, or Confucianism, all Buddhist believe that there are four Noble Truths; and this can be said is the basis of Buddha-Dharma. The truths are as follows:

a. *Life means suffering*

This was Buddha's way of saying "life sucks; deal with it". The question here should be how badly does it suck? *Well, that all depends on how well or how poorly we deal with life's mishaps and misfortunes.*

In actually life is full of joys as well as suffering; but it just seems that the moments of joy are by far fewer and shorter than the moments of suffering that we experience our lives. Buddha discovered early on his journey that to live means to suffer and no one absolutely no one is an exception to this. As babies we suffered simply because we existed and because we're helpless. Have you ever been on a flight with a crying screaming baby? As adults we know how awful it feels when our ears plugged up, imagine the feeling of a poor child not knowing what's going on and being completely helpless to make it better. If we feel uncomfortable and we chew gum or hold our breath till our ears adjust back to normal, but what can infant do? Well, nothing except scream and cry and hope that someone well help and make it stop.

If you are asking yourself "Why is all life suffering and not happiness all the time?" Well, the answer is simple; it is because we are human and because we are full of flaws and imperfections. The world that we live in is imperfect and that is why we encounter all sorts of suffering in our lives. We suffer physically, psychologically and emotionally. Our levels of suffering range from slight discomforts like an itchy on the nose to the deepest most sorrowful hurting a person can experience like losing a loved one.

Our physical suffering includes pains, illnesses, stressing, worrying, aging and ultimately dying. However our suffering goes beyond just the physical we also endure all sorts of psychological suffering. These include our fears, our emotions like sadness, depression, worrying and the frustrations that stem from jealousy, envy and other misdirected passions.

Luckily for us there is a flipside to life and though absurd at times, life is beautiful. Just as life offers us our fair share of suffering it also offers us the most wonderful moments of our lives; these are our joyful, happy moments; the opposite of when we are suffering. They are the wonderful feelings and emotions that we experience, like falling in love, having wealth, feeling secure and powerful, in general the feelings of joy and happiness. The catch to this is that our happiness is temporary; we have it for moments or on occasions throughout our life but it isn't something that we can keep forever and ever. The joys we experience in our life give us great pleasures and likewise these very joys can be evil when they are gone. Happiness and joy is something like a flickering light it can brighten a dark room but it is so fragile that with any turbulence it can easily be blown out. We can never know how long those happy moments will last. This means that although getting what we want and feeling happy is attainable, it's not permanent, without exception happy moments pass. Everything passes including our loved ones and ourselves. It happens to everyone and no one can escape it no matter how strong a person they may be, I mean come on even Batman lost Robin, absolutely everything and everyone passes.

Certainly throughout our lifetime we all have our ups and downs, as they say "we win some we loose some", however, life becomes a constant struggle to get what we want and sometimes we tire ourselves doing so. We become obsessed with our desires whether it is to have the best toys like the fancy car, the huge home and the perfect partner, whatever our desires may be we can get what we want but we cannot keep what we want forever, or once we have something we may not wanted it anymore, hence the cycle of frustration and suffering. Great jobs come and go, love fades, and people get sick, things change, whatever. Change is inevitable it happens and none of us are immune to it, whether it's a series of lay off or younger competitors pushing us out, all good things come to an end.

Even love fades or ceases to exist, just look at the current divorce rate in the United States, approximately 51% of all marriages end in divorce, which means that it is likely that a less than rock solid relationship will fail. Let's look at the best-case scenario were two kindred spirits find each other. At some point life will separate the two because no love, no matter how great escapes death. Eventually everything comes to an end. And yes believe it or not we choose this suffering, perhaps because the good that comes from it is worth the sorrow that we may endure at some point. Another reason could be because of the lack of experience; therefore we want this type of attachment. Remember attachment to anything will cause us suffering.

6. The origin of suffering is desire

This is Buddha's ways of saying "how does it feel to want?" *Well, it feels pretty bad doesn't it? Especially when we don't get what we want, right?*

As children we've all had one of those moments when we see another kid eating an ice cream or a candy bar and suddenly we want exactly whatever it is that they have. Naturally we ask mom or dad if we can have one and they say "NO". Throughout our life we have that same feeling every single time we desire something that is out of reach; that's why the origin of our suffering is desire. The more we want the more we suffer.

All of our suffering is caused by our desires and by our attachment to material things or to circumstances and ideas. Our suffering stems from ignorance and our lack of understanding of how and why our minds get attached to material objects, to ideas, and conditions. Our desires include material objects like fancy clothing, expensive cars, and all sorts of gadgets; however, we also suffer because of our attachment to ideas and because we don't let things go. How many of us still hate the first guy or girl that broke our little heart? Yes, the very first one way back in the 1st grade, the one we can't think about without twitching or getting a little aggravated. Well, I am exaggerating about the kid in the first grade but lets talk about a few boyfriends down the line, why do we hold on to the moments that we shared with that person, why do we insist on holding a grudge or any other feelings towards that person? Well again because we are human and because we are flawed and because we become fixated on an idea about how our lives should be and whom we should share it with. Another examples of becoming fixated on ideas is something like wanting for be rich, or having the desire to feel important, or wishing that others find us irresistibly sexy, whatever the case may be, our self perception causes us a great deal of suffering, particularly when our self perception and reality don't match. In short the more want the more we suffer.

And although any of these things that we strive for may bring us great pleasure, they will also come with a certain degree of stress factors. For instance, if one gets 15 minutes of fame, then we want another 15 minutes of fame, which causes to us seek more of that fame; it's kind of like eating a piece of chocolate cake shortly there after we want another piece of chocolate cake, which can makes us fat if we over indulge in our desire. Then we're trapped by the very thing that brought us so much joy. It becomes a never-ending cycle of suffering. Socrates once said desire is like an itch, if you scratch it you will feel relief but the moment you stop scratching you'll begin to feel discomfort and anxiety and the desire to scratch again. It is better not to scratch, as it would be better not to have the desire at all.

In the movie Mean Girls, Cady once said about her archrival Regina George…"The weird thing about hanging out with Regina was that I could hate her, and at the same time, I still wanted her to like me."

Isn't it always like that? We always want what we can't have; we want what others have.

c. *The cessation of suffering is attainable*

Buddha's way of saying "Get over it…" *And yes, we actually can get over it!*

The wonderful news about the nature of our suffering is that we can attain the cessation of suffering. If we become enlightened we can control our suffering by learning how to control our desires. We can manage to bring our suffering to an end. In order to do this we must undergo nirodha, which means to undo our cravings and our attachments; this can be achieved through a series of meditation techniques that take us back through every experience and every desire that we have ever felt until we get to the source of our suffering. Who knows how far back that can be? Any how Nirodha is something like letting things go kind of like "whatever"; you go back, you experience it, you make amends and you let it go. After that our desires become less powerful a good example would be like knowing there's something behind door number one but moving on without stopping to have to look because we are already content with what we have. Isn't that liberating? To know there is something there but being content enough with ourselves and our own spirituality that whatever maybe behind door no. 1 won't change us. Nirodha basically extinguishes all forms of

cara rios

wants and desires. The formula to overcoming our suffering is by attaining dispassion towards our desires in other words the cessation of suffering is to "Get over it!"

The ultimate dispassion and freedom from attachments is called Nirvana. Nirvana is not like being in trance but it is being completely disconnected of any desires. Nirvana is being in a state of nothingness free of worries, troubles, complexities, fabrications and ideas. It is like being in a state of "Whatever" in other words it is being completely "Chill".

d. There is a path to the cessation of suffering

The path to end our suffering is the Road to Whatever, which can be achieved through moderation and by following the eightfold path. Luckily of us Buddha didn't give us the bad news about the human condition and the cycle of suffering without showing us how to deal with it. It's certainly not a quick easy fix however; the path to ending our suffering is a gradual path of self-improvement. Buddha taught us what is called the Eightfold Path, which is the middle road. It is the middle between the extremes of excessive self-indulgence and excessive self-mortification; for our purpose the road to whatever is the middle road as whatever is ambiguous or sort of in the middle. The eightfold path is composed of the following steps: right thought, right intention, right speech, right action, right livelihood, right effort, right mindfulness and right concentration.

When talking about right thought consider that reality is created in our minds. It is said that right thought is the beginning and the end of the path because everything starts there and ends there in our minds. When we focus on right thought and not stray from the outcomes that we desire there is no stopping us. However, right thought is not only positive thinking; it also includes avoiding thinking harmful thoughts. We sew what we reap and our thoughts are the seeds and our mind is the garden so keep them positive.

Right thought is being sure in your mind as well as in your heart about what we want. Remember the movie "Shallow Hall" (2001) staring Jack Black and Gwyneth Paltro? After Hal gets hypnotized he sort of ends up in a state of right view as he could only see people for who they were on the inside regardless of what they look like on the outside. That's the reason why he couldn't see Rosemary Shanahan as a fat wall flower because he could only see her as she was on the inside a beautiful caring vibrant young woman. He was in a state of right view and was able to see beyond the visible. When his friend Mauricio questions Hal about his fascination with Rosemary this is what he said.

Hal asks: *Okay, who do you think is the most beautiful woman in the world?*

Mauricio replies: Wonder Woman.

Then Hal say: *Okay, let's say everyone else in the world thought Wonder Woman was ugly.*

Mauricio say: It wouldn't matter. Because I know they'd be wrong.

Aha Hal says: *See! That's what I had with Rosemary! I saw a knock out, I don't care what anybody else saw!*

In essence we control our reality by what we think; our reality does not control us unless we believe it does and allow it too. But it is only through right view that it goes beyond an intellectual capacity just as wisdom is more than knowledge it is a total awareness of our surroundings and of our feelings. Right view includes both what we can see and what we can't see. In Shallow Hal's case the state of hypnosis that he was in made him ultra aware beyond skin deep.

In talking about right intention, let's say that right intention is to act out of kindness, love and compassion toward all beings. Right intention is what heroes and heroines are made of, they do what they do because they have right intention and not for the glory, the money or the fame. You will see that as we dive into lives of the gals in these flicks we'll see that though these gals maybe misguided at times for the most part they have right intention. These heroines are on their own path to self discovery and it is only through right intention that they manage to make things right for themselves and everyone else.

Let's talk about right speech. Consider that right speech again is an act of love and compassion similar to right thought and right intention. Speaking is a privilege therefore we should try to avoid doing harm towards other with our gift of speech. We should avoid lying and using harmful words towards others as well as partaking in gossip. How, many times have you been in a great mood when suddenly someone drags you into some gossip and by the end of the conversation you're as upset as the person who dragged you into the conversation, when you have no involvement in the situation? You end up upset by the mere act of listening to all the drama. Nothing good comes out of gossip therefore we should avoid getting involved whenever possible. Cady Herron of Mean Girls saw first had the turmoil that gossip can cause. Here are her thoughts on the matter. *"Calling somebody else fat won't make you any skinnier. Calling someone stupid doesn't make you any smarter. And ruining Regina George's life definitely didn't make me any happier. All you can do in life is try to solve the problem in front of you."*

Right Action is a little different than the other steps here we must actually take the steps to do the right thing. The hard part of this step is that often times we aren't sure what doing the right thing really means. Doing the right thing can means a lot of things to a lot of different people. Remember the Spike Lee's film "Do the Right Thing"? The right thing was one thing for the Italians and something else altogether for the African Americans and something else for the Porto Ricans, but in the end it was the same thing for all of them they all had the exact same struggle each trying to find there place. Though they were fighting each other the entire time they really needed to be united as each of the groups were oppressed by the same circumstances. Not one group was better than the other but they believed that they were and that created the stress between all the groups. They couldn't see that they were just one group and that they really needed each other if they could ever survive. It is one thing to think positively but it is something altogether different to act positively and right action is about doing the right thing. Right action is like the follow through on a promise or intention. It is one thing to say we are going to do x, y or z, but it is something altogether to do it.

In talking about right livelihood consider living in a state of compassion, basically avoiding activities that cause damage and hurt others. Right livelihood includes using all of the prior steps as they are link are and cross over. For instance you cannot have right livelihood if you do not have right view and right thought; we must think positively in order to behave positively.

The idea of right concentration is that we are on the path to peace when we are focused on right concentration. A good analogy would be a walk in the woods and not getting of the beaten track, just staying focused on where you want to go; when walking in the woods the drama always begins the minutes someone gets off the beaten path. It's like every scary movie I have ever seen. Something bad always happens when someone leaves the room. In life there will always temptations and other distractions that can lead us astray from our goal but when we have right concentration we know where we currently stand and where we are headed and everything that lies between here and there. On the path of right concentration we may stumble from time to time but with a focused mind we get up and move on. With right concentration we can see why we have fallen and over what stone we have tripped and we can watchfully continue on our road. Life is a never ending series of test and without a doubt we will fail at some of these tests; however the goal isn't to pass every single one but sometimes to learn from them. If we learn even if we have failed we win.

Chapter 3:

Legally Whatever
(The Awakened Material Girl)

"All people see when they look at me is blonde hair and big boobs." Elle Woods

Robert Luketic's 2001 movie Legally Blonde, staring Reese Witherspoon is a perfect example of what Buddhists call finding your Tao, which translates to finding your path. In Legally Blond, Elle Woods is a Belle Air socialite that is completely clueless about who she is and about what she would like to become. She's like raw piece of marble wanting to become Michael Angelo's David. At the beginning she is big piece of marble waiting to become something, the possibilities of what that piece of marble can become are endless for instance it can become beautiful piece of furniture or a grand monument; in reality a block of marble can become almost anything once it finds its path, it's Tao or it's "Whatever", it can become anything including just staying a piece of marble.

At the beginning of the movie Elle is the typical Belle Air material girl, blonde, stacked, and wealthy. She is perky, pretty, and wears nothing but pink designer clothing; she even has a matching Chihuahua purse dog. Elle seems to be completely self-absorbed only concerned with fashion, make-up, her small circle of sorority sisters and her boyfriend. She's the girl we all love to hate, she's the girl that has it all; the rich girl that is way too perky, way too perfect and far too privileged. Outwardly everyone hates people like Elle Woods, but inwardly most people envy people like Elle, even if just a little. I mean come on it would be nice to be in her overpriced Gucci shoes, even if just for a day? Of course it would be, but since we are not it is our human nature to build a certain aversion towards people like this and when we meet people like this in real world we just think to ourselves or murmur among our friends "She thinks she's all that!"

Not only is Elle a total snob, she also lacks life experience as her point of reference is so narrow. The girl lives in a Barbie like world with Barbie friends and all the matching accessories and the one thing Elle loves best is fashion. She has a remarkable memory and can remember endless details about fashion at the drop of a hat. To suite her perfect life, Elle even has a perfect boyfriend Warren Huntington the 3rd; together they make the ideal Barbie & Ken couple. He's a handsome young man that comes from a well to do family and to top it all off he's just been accepted at Harvard School of Law.

One night during an intimate dinner with Warner, Elle is expecting Warren to pop the big question; however Warner only surprises her by breaking up with her. He explains.

"See Pooh bear, now that I have been accepted to Harvard Law, I have to stop dicking around."

Elle perks up thinking he means that he wants to settle down and marry her, Warren continues, "I mean if I am gonna become a senator by the time I'm 30; I have to marry a Jackie not a Marilyn"

Ouch, he called her an airhead; that was just rude! The poor girl was completely shattered over the breakup. She practically had a mental break down. In her desperation Elle set forth to win back his love and she knew exactly how she would do it. Elle decides to become the perfect Jackie, worthy of Warren's love. To be near him till she can win him back she decides to pursue a Law degree at Harvard.

When she gets the crazy idea of going to Harvard Law in pursuit of Warren, she tells her dad I'm going to Harvard. Her dad says: "Law school is for boring, ugly, serious people and you button are none of those things".

As the story unfolds Elle struggles with the dichotomy of what she is and of what she wants to become. If Elle is ever going to achieve her goal she'll need right concentration. In the process of chasing Warren she undergoes a major change and endures all sorts so suffering and humiliations trying fit into a circle in which she's had no intention of ever being a part of. She tries her best to please her Harvard colleagues and fails profoundly after all she's a HOTTIE not a NERD. It is as if Elle looses her essence in order to impress those around her including the now ex-boyfriend that she's trying to win back.

In her attempts to gain the respect of her colleagues she alters her looks, changes her study habits and she even finds

17

support in the most unlikely of friends. Elle becomes really good friends with the nail shop girl, but in spite of her multiple unsuccessful attempts to impress the Harvard snottiest, she has strong will and manages to fumble her way through her first year at Harvard Law. At the end of that year she even earns herself an internship at a very prestigious Law Firms, beating out a couple of her colleagues for the position. You Go Girl!

In spite of her huge transformation, it is still Elle's essence and love of fashion that wins her, her first case. At the point when Elle becomes true to herself, she begins to get cut a little slack from her colleagues. When Elle finally gets into her "Whatever" mode and stops caring about impressing her colleagues and begins to trust her instincts, she achieves a higher level of nirodha, she stops caring about what others think about her. Surprisingly even to herself she's not as stupid as everyone thought, in fact quite the contrary, she's sharp as a tack. Somehow when she starts acting like herself again, she's the same as before, but not the same. Her experience in walking in the outcast, misfit's shoes has made her a better person. We become one with Elle, because she's now crossed over and has fallen from her grace and privilege and has felt the stuff that we all go through, pain, heartache and humiliation. The same as Buddha did over 25,000 years ago Elle becomes the awaked material girl. See the similarities in Prince Siddhartha's journey and Elle's situation?

Elle is assigned a murder case that the key eyewitness against Elle's client is a hot Latin pool boy. He claims to be having an affair with the defendant a young, successful "Workout Guru" (which Elle adores and follows religiously). The workout guru is being accused of murdering her own husband, a wealthy old fart. The thing is that she had no reason or motive to do it; she had her own money and apparently really loved the guy.

"I just don't think that Brooke could've done this. Exercise gives you endorphins. Endorphins make you happy. Happy people just don't shoot their husbands, they just don't." says Elle

During the trial the Pool boy makes the gruesome mistake of mocks Elle's shoes. He says. "Don't stomp your last season Prada shoes at me, honey."

Uh how dare he? She realizes then that the pool guy is gay; because only a gay man would be able to quote that kind of fashion details and be correct. She figures that there is no possible way he could be having an affair with her client because he's gay. During the trial she throws out a series of fashion questions to the guy and then sneaks in "What's your boyfriend's name?" To which he replies emphatically "Rodrigo!" Ops, they guy is busted!

It's Elle's Tao, her whatever, her essence and natural inclinations that wins her the case. It is only when she says "Whatever" to everything around her, and disregards her fears and gains the courage to follow her heart that she finds the truth that she has been seeking. She discovers the truth about the case and wins it, but more importantly she discovers the truth about Elle Wood and the powers she holds within. See all along her problem was not getting back her ex-boyfriend but rather finding her true self. It was figuring out what that the piece of marble wanted to become and in Elle's case it wanted to be a damn brilliant lawyer.

Elle is a great example of what anyone of us can accomplish once we have set our mind to it and once we have discover and begin to practice right view. When we begin to believe in ourselves and begin to expect more of ourselves we can achieve great things. Every single person is different therefore every single path is different, whether it is to becoming an attorney or to be an artist, a singer, or being a contortionist at the circus, when we find our path and our road to whatever there is no obstacle that can get in our way.

Interpretation:

The message here is that no matter how hard you try you can never be something you are not. We all have a purpose here and the more that we resist it the more we suffer for it. When Warren broke up with Elle he was sure that she wasn't the girl for him and no amount of Elle's merits would change that.

On the other hand Elle herself regardless of whether or not she believed it, she was a woman that knew how to get what she wanted; she just had to figure out exactly what she wanted. She discovered that what she wanted to was to grow, to change and to become a better person than the person she was at the beginning. I believe that we all want to grow and become better than what we are now and that we have been in that past; I mean there is always room for improvement; however few of us dare to step out of our comforts zones in pursuit of our happiness. The message here is that we have figure out what we want and then go after it.

Chapter 4:

The Zen of the Mean Girls "You're such a plastics"

"Okay, I'm going to forgive you because I'm a very Zen person and I'm on a lot of pain medication right now"… Regina George

The 2004 American teen comedy film Mean Girls, written by Tina Fey and directed by Mark Waters perfectly reflects western society's value system and people's behavior toward each other. High school is all about Queen Bees and Wannabees and the competitive world we live in is a reflection of your typical high school as people will do whatever it takes to be popular, to be the best, to feel important regardless of how many people they hurt in the process. Though Mean Girl takes place at Beverly Hills high school, the cattiness the girls dish out towards each other can be seen in many facets of life, like the office, a nightclub, at the gym or wherever. The good thing about recognizing meanness when it happens is that we all have the choice not to engage in it. Once we realize that our actions truly are dictated by our own free will we can then take the responsibility for the way we behave and we can change the things we don't like about our behaviors. The beauty of life is that anyone can change anything they want about ourselves regardless of how weak or how powerful we believe ourselves to be.

In Mean Girls Caddy Herron staring Lindsey Loham represents the underdog, however, in spite of being the new kid on the block Caddy manages to teach Regina George, the meanest girl in school, a good lesson about the power of Zen. Caddy shows us how the new kid on the block can find the courage to confront and battle the most popular girl in school. I think most of us can relate to Caddy because at the beginning of the movie she's sort of a plain Jane and we feel sorry for her in a way. She's that girl that we may have been at one point or another in our lives; the shy girl, the nerdy girl, the girl who gets pushed around because she's a dork, but that later becomes as hot as an American Idol, or the fat girl who never got invited to the prom and later becomes a rock star. We all want Cady to win; just as in life the world wants redemption for the oppressed, because if they win it's a victory for all of humanity. When the underdog wins it is a confirmation that any one can thrive under any circumstance including as the new kid on the block.

In Mean Girls as in life we want the little fish to win because their victories inspire us to dream, to believe that anything is possible and to accomplish regardless of how impossible or difficult the task at hand may seem. I mean come on if the new kid on the block can face up to the "Plastics" then guess what each and everyone one of us can face up to our challenges, whatever they may be and with a little will and discipline we can overcome them.

As humans we are full of flaws; in fact psychology studies have shown that human beings we are not naturally inclined to do the good. Goodness is a quality that has been taught to us and passed down through the generations. It has been ingrained in our value system that good must always prevail over evil and that the interruption of the good can only bring about an imbalance in the Yin-Yang. The Yin-Yan is an East Asian thought, that two complementary forces or principles that make up all aspects of life. The Yin is earth, female, dark, passive, and absorbing; it is present in even numbers and in valleys and streams and is represented by the tiger. While the Yang is heaven, male, light, active, and penetrating; it is present in odd numbers and mountains and is represented by the dragon, but together they express the interdependence of opposites. The same as in mean girls the cool kids aren't cool unless the wannabee kids think so.

Ironically in Buddhism unlike in Western culture where the richer get richer and the strong always win, in Buddha-Dharma it's the little guy who has the greatest opportunity for growth. The underdog has the chance to become greater than he or she is at the beginning. In the end the less significant character becomes more significant by applying right intention towards others. This person accomplishes what he or she does by right concentration and not straying from their path and by not letting their ego get the best of them. Although this person may remain the same by then end they are enlightened. They are the same but different. This person gets to be in another persons skin and usually comes face to face with having the power to destroy his or her opponent but opts not to out of kindness, unlike the privileged the underdog, when given the opportunity for change they willing to accept it.

cara rios

An excellent example of this dichotomy; of the earthly and the celestial is Cady's arrival at Beverly Hills High. This is Cady's first time in a public school and completely oblivious to the concept of "Cool". After hanging out with a Janis the Gothic chick and a fat boy named Damian for a few days, Cady quickly learns the ins and outs of the high school scene and in no time Cady builds a desire to be cool, to be admired and to be adored; she knows who's on the A-List is and wants her part of it.

Both Janis and Damian like everyone one else at school have at some point been humiliated by the mean girls, so they decided to use Cady to try to get back at them. The three outcasts Cady, Janis and Damian plan to destroy the plastics. It involves Cady going undercover as one of them and in a few days Cady ends up in cahoots with "The Plastics". These girls "the Plastics" as they are know around school are the prettiest, most popular and meanest girls in school. They get off on hurting others for no reason except their personal vanity. Here is how Janis whom at one was Regina George's best friend describes her. She tells Cady:

> *"evil takes a human form in Regina George. Don't be fooled because she may seem like your typical selfish, back-stabbing slut faced ho-bag, but in reality, she's so much more than that"*

In spite of the Janis's warnings to Cady about Regina, Cady still gets her 15 minutes of high school fame and in the process she ends up going through a major change. She goes from being a sweet kid to becoming a total heartless cruel material girl; she becomes a "PLASTIC" and manages to alienate her real friends Janis and the fat boy. The ironic thing about the whole situation is that deep in her heart Cady knows that what she is striving for is something that has no real significance to her or anybody else, however, as stupid as it may be to become popular she can't help but to wanted to be cool. See the link to

Buddhism? Our desires are the basis of our suffering and Cady is about to open up a huge can of it.

The original plan fails them; instead of getting back at the plastics they create a monster and her name is Cady Herron. Cady's sudden change surprised everyone, her friends, her parents, even the mean girls; she becomes a horrible person; she becomes completely self-centered and begins caring only about herself. Cady's role play went too far; she becomes what she was trying to destroy. Cady steps over the people who care about her. Now Cady begins to perpetuate what the mean girls had started. She too begins hurting others in order to make herself look and feel good.

Here is what Cady says to Janis about not inviting her to her house party. *"You know I couldn't invite you! I had to pretend to be plastic."*

And Janis replies *"Hey, buddy, you're not pretending anymore! You're plastic! Cold, shiny, hard plastic!"*

Its true Cady had turned into meanest plastic of all. The burn book was the final draw for Cady. The burn book is where the mean girls write down all the rumors they have start about people that have fallen out of their grace. They write rumors about people they wanted to humiliate and destroy. The burn book is full of cruel, hateful things that are for the most part not true. Nonetheless what's written in the burn book whether true or not still has the power to stigmatize those on the receiving end, sometimes for years to come. Cady truly crosses over from pretending to be a plastic to truly becoming a plastic when she starts adding things to the burn book. Cady knows how powerful and how unforgiving the words written in the burn book can be, but still she writes an ugly rumor about her nemeses Regina George. That's when Regina figures out Cady's true intentions are to replace her as the queen bee and end up with Regina's ex-boyfriend; Regina's revenge would be brutal.

Regina made copies of the book and posted them all over the high school, later running off to the principles office to accuse Cady and her clan. The school was in complete chaos; at that point Cady realized what she had caused. She realizes all the people that she has hurt and all because she was obsessed with being cool. This was the awakening moment for Cady; it was her opportunity to make things right again, but how? Everyone hated her, she had trespassed on so many people, how could they trust her again?

The thing is that just as people change for the bad, sometimes people change for the good. Cady's experiences with her desire for fame taught her a very valuable lesson that people's feelings are far more important than being cool. She spent the next few weeks laying low and trying to repair some of the damage she had caused. At the prom, which she only attended as a volunteer worker helping serve refreshments and stuff she was announced Prom Queen. Cady accepted the crown only to perform the ultimate sacrifice. She broke the plastic tiara into a dozen pieces then started sharing the bits with every girl in room including Regina George. It is at this point that Cady makes her way back. She is finally as she was at the beginning but now enlighten, the same as Buddha, the same as Elle Woods and the same as anyone one of us who have at some point lost our way and then found our way back.

When Cady becomes enlightened a little voice in her head resonates with the lesson she has just learned. It says *"Calling somebody else fat won't make you any skinnier. Calling someone stupid doesn't make you any smarter. And ruining Regina George's life definitely didn't make me any happier. All you can do in life is try to solve the problem in front of you."*

See how much better of a person she is now? Although she doesn't manage to destroy Regina George as she intended nor does she get the boy; but she did get a chance to take a stroll in Regina George's shoes. Cady has now been on the other side and has seen that being there is not as fun as it's cracked out to be. A lot of dirty work goes into being a plastic, like humiliating and hurting people. Just like the young prince at the beginning of the book, Cady realizes that what she really wants more than anything is to be a simple happy girl, and that's what she becomes.

Interpretation:

The lesson to be learned from Mean Girls is that the more we want to be something that we are not, the more we end up hurting ourselves and others along the way. Caddy knew throughout her entire journey that what she was doing was hurting a lot of people. Luckily she realized that losing her essence in the name of popularity was far too steep of a price for high school popularity. This experience makes Cady better because it humbled her and made her stronger and more human because now she has been on both sides and knows how cruel either side can be. In order to come enlightened we all have to get to a point where understanding another person perspective; we have to learn that is it not all about you but all about us all the time. Just like Cady realized that every girl at the prom deserved a piece of tiara because they were all in the same boat. Not one was more important than another and this is an elemental in Buddhism, hence the reason that most Buddhists are vegetarian. I am not suggesting that we must all become vegetarians in order to become enlightened but we should consider that each living thing is as important as another and here for a reason.

Chapter 5

Buddha's Delight

"forget about your past life cause this could be our last life; we're gonna reach nirvana" ... Cora Corman

The 2007 film Music and Lyrics helps us define STRENGTH as it is viewed in Buddhism. Strength is not about having super power or about having the ability to forcefully make someone do something against his or her own will but rather it is about the ability to do something over and over again in an almost perfect sequence every time. Our strengths are the characteristics that that we have a natural inclination towards, like birds chirping in the morning or a roster ka-ka-doodling at sunrise. The things we love doing ant that we do almost effortlessly and nearly perfectly each time. For people similarly to the animals that live in nature; people who can do what they are best suited for usually find success and tranquility in their actions. If you are a feline you hunt, if you are a vulture you scavenger and so on. For us when dealing with the everyday life situations and difficulties, we better manage them when we tap into our personal strengths. Funny people get ahead by making other people like them, bullies push people around and they get around that way, while charming people get virtually whatever they want by engaging people in their needs and wants.

In Music and Lyrics, I found the perfect example of a young artist dealing with her anxiety about fame and fortune by doing what she knew how to do best, simply dancing. The film staring Huge Grant as Alex Fletcher a has-been musician and Drew Barrymore as Sophie Fisher, the zany artist girl struggling to make her way; the two find each other and partner up to write rhythm and lyrics for a talented young Diva named Cora Corman. Alex and Sophie teach each other a few lessons about life and friendship while trying meet Cora's deadline for a new song. In fact, everyone in the film learns from each other and both Alex and Sophie learn from Cora, who at first glance seems to be a self centered little brat child star, but when they get to know her better they see she's quite a stoic young woman; who takes things for what they are and without much emotion. Cora doesn't take too much sympathy on her composers, instead when she's not happy about their work she simply discards like its nothing to her and moves on and goes right back to what works for her and what she likes; hip hop. Cora loves dancing hip hop because it is her escape from all of life's problems.

Alex who's been a singer and artist long before Cora was born, feels that insulted by Cora attitude towards his work. When Alex finally builds up the courage to confront her about her disrespectful actions towards Sophie and him, and about they way she has been treating them as if they were virtually

29

are non-existent,   Cora stops him dead cold in the middle of his outburst.

She says to Alex: *"Do you have an idea what it's like to be 16 years old and to have an entire industry depending on you? To go through your parents divorce and to be put in the middle like a token and to have no one in the world to turn to?"*

He's speechless; she continues: *"You know how I deal with it?"*

Again Alex is speechless. She then says: *"I dance, I dance because that is what I know how to do, because it is what keeps me from going insane!"*

Suddenly there's a new light shed on Cora and though she is young they now see that she has life experience. When he realizes that other people including perfect little Miss Cora have bigger problems that him he re-evaluates his life and suddenly, his ego isn't as big and important as it was. Alex and Sophie go back to the drawing board to write Cora's song and they finally hit it. In the meantime they encounter another problem; they are in love with each other and neither one of them knows what to do about it. They're both scared, oh what mess! People always manage to hurt each other because we are human and because we carry a lifetime of scars and these two are not exception they both have their own set of baggage.

Though they manage to get the song to Cora in time for her big concert they end up having a terrible falling out. Sophie is miserable because she feels betrayed by Alex, both professionally and romantically as Alex starts acting like a total egotistical idiot. He takes full credit for the song that they wrote together and not only that but he starts hiding from her trying to avoid talking about what happened between them. He basically leaves Sophie in the dark without any kind of explanation about how he's acting towards her. Perhaps he himself doesn't even really understand what's going on, perhaps he's scared too. Nonetheless he really manages to let Sophie down.

By Cora's big concert Alex gets an opportunity to make things right. He gets the chance to put the eightfold path into action and to change the outcomes for himself and for those that have helped him along the way. It's up to Alex to do the right thing and to own up to his commitments to Sophie and Cora. Once he starts to feel in his heart the trouble that he has stirred up; his nature brings him around to do the right thing. He begins his walking on the eightfold path. The wonderful thing about free will is that just as we have the free will to really mess things up we also have the free will to fix things and to turn things around and that's what Alex does. Somehow he arranges with Cora to sing a duo with her at her big concert. When he gets up he makes things right for Sophie, he dedicates the song they wrote together to her and gives her the credit she deserved. He also finally shows her his true self and goes back to being the sweet loving guy the entire movie theater fell in love with.

Interpretation:

The lesson here is that the truer we are to ourselves the truer we can be to those around us. Cora kept her Zen by doing what she knew how to do best; she danced because it was her nature. She never lost her cool, even under the most stressful situations a young woman can encounter, because her "whatever" attitude helped her stay in control. Her cool also helped Alex and Sophie get back in their Zen as writers, as friends and as lovers.

The beauty about finding our path and sticking to it is that in doing so we don't only elevate ourselves but we also help elevate everyone that we are connected to. And ultimately we are connected to everyone in one way or another. Imagine every person that you have ever met in your life, whether they have made an impact or not the likelihood of two lives crossing with over 9 billion inhabitants in the world are very slim! Figure that those people that manage to cross our paths and vice versa must give each other a human experience. We know humanity as we see it in others, for that reason its best to keep things real at all times because our actions will without a doubt impact others like a domino effect. "Be kind whenever possible. It is always possible" Dalai Lama

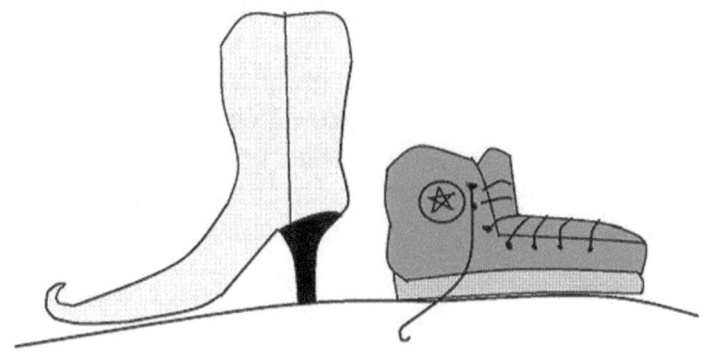

Chapter 6:

The Devil Wears Prada & Buddha Wears Whatever!

"Happiness is not something ready made. It comes from your own actions." His Holiness the Dalai Lama

The 2006 comedy drama the Devil Wears Prada, directed by David Frankel is a film that revels in pleasure: the pleasure of fashion, luxury, power and ambition. The film is about Andrea Sachs (played by Annie Hathaway) a small town journalist who lands a great job in the fashion world of NYC in search of her big break. Andy manages to score the job that a million girls would kill for; she becomes the assistant to one of the biggest magazine editors in NYC, the ruthless and cynical Miranda Priestly played by Meryl Streep (the terrible). Andy delighted with her new assignment sets out on the adventure of her life; she intends to make a name for herself in the rough, tough and dirty world of high fashion. But the lessons she ends up learning are all together different than she expected; she learns about greed and ambition and even get a chance to meet face to face with her own ugly side. She learns how people act and how far people will go for power and prestige. She also learns about staying true to oneself and about loyalty.

Becoming the assistant to *Runway's* top fashion editor is a dream come true for Andy, after all it's her big break and as Frank Sinatra would say "if you can make it here she can make it anywhere." Small town girl, big city, new job, sounds dreamy right? Well, in no time, Andy's dream job turns out to be a very grave nightmare. She realizes at the very beginning that she's nothing like the fashion divas at *Runway* magazine. She's simple; she's doesn't follow fashion; she's genuinely nice and the kind of person that doesn't take herself too serious. Imagine her awkwardness around the vamps at *Runway*. They immediately made her the escape goat, she becomes *Runway's* Cinderella getting pushed around by everyone "Andy get me a mocha; Andy fetch me those swatches; Andy this and Andy that" and absolutely everything that can possibly go wrong is Andyyyyy's fault! The people at runway are so caught up in their personal conspicuous lives that they don't have a moment to show a glimpse of kindness towards another person. Runway is the type of environment that takes a sweet girl like Andy, chews them up and spites them out bitter old bags like the rest them. In Andy's case they attempt to strip her of any glimpse of self esteem the girl has, they try destroy it. The people at Runway are a pretty sorry bunch, but what more can be expected of the fashion world? We're talking about the industry that has made its mark by making people feel fat and ugly, only to turn around to sell them the antidote; beauty and glamour in a bottle. Miranda Presley however, goes beyond mean she's outright monstrous. She never misses a chance to cut the poor girl down and to humiliate her in the cruelest ways. Andy once made the mistake of snickering while Miranda and her assistants where debating on which of two identical belts to put on an outfit.

Miranda said "Something funny?"

Andy innocently replied "No, no, nothing. Y'know, it's just that both those belts look exactly the same to me. Y'know, I'm still learning about all this stuff."

Here's what happens next. "This... stuff'? Oh... ok. I see, you think this has nothing to do with you. You go to your closet and you select out, oh I don't know, that lumpy blue sweater, for instance, because you're trying to tell the world that you take yourself too seriously to care about what you put on your back. But what you don't know is that that sweater is not just blue, it's not turquoise, it's not lapis, it's actually cerulean. You're also blithely unaware of the fact that in 2002, Oscar De La Renta did a collection of cerulean gowns. And then I think it was Yves St Laurent, wasn't it, who showed cerulean military jackets? And then cerulean quickly showed up in the collections of 8 different designers. Then it filtered down through the department stores and then trickled on down into some tragic casual corner where you, no doubt, fished it out of some clearance bin.

However, that blue represents millions of dollars and countless jobs and so it's sort of comical how you think that you've made a choice that exempts you from the fashion industry when, in fact, you're wearing the sweater that was selected for you by the people in this room. From a pile of stuff."
Miranda Priestly

Now that was straight up COLD BLOODED! The only way Andy would be able to withstand the abuse that got thrown at her would be to find her strength in "Whatever" including in learning from Miranda. Believe it or not Miranda Presley has found her own whatever, grim as it may be Miranda knows exactly who and what she is and so does everyone around her. I mean come on, how many of us have encountered people like Miranda in our lives; strong women that don't have to please others to get their way; they just get their way. Miranda is sure of her whatever, she is extreme and arrogant; nonetheless she knows who she is, everyone does! And although Andy may be a little scared of Miranda, she does admire her, she once stuck up for her when the other girls were bad mouthing Miranda. She said

"If she were a man, the only thing people would talk about is how good she is at her job." Andy

Lucky for Andy, life always offers her a guiding light; some balance; it's what they call the "Yin-Yang" the good and the bad. If you there is death then there is life, if there is darkness then there is life, when there is a storm then there is calm. For Andy it's Nigel the magazine fashion director who shows a little pity towards Andy; he takes her under his wing. Nigel becomes her friend and mentor; he even gives her a makeover, turning her into a fashion diva to perfectly fit for her new job. But what Nigel does for Andy is more than just a make over it's an entire overhaul her whole person; her confidence goes up. She becomes more aggressive to the point that she gets caught up in looking the part, and in playing the part. Andy actually becomes the part; sweet little Andy starts a little mean and hold hearted herself... It's not personal its just business. In fact her new attitude is so fierce that she begins acting as vicious towards people who care about her as Miranda Presley. She begins doing whatever it takes and stepping over anyone to get what she wants. I think she crosses the line from having a health ambition to becoming a full on rat when she ruins her relationship with her father, then picks her career over the relationship with her boyfriend. She becomes ambitions to the point of betraying Emily, Miranda's previous assistant. At one point in her efforts of winning Miranda over, Andy manages to steals away her friend Emily's chance to go to Paris for a fashion convention, the one thing Emily had been working towards all year long.

> *Andy Sachs: Emily. You look so thin.*
> *Emily: Really? It's for Paris, I'm on this new diet. Well, I don't eat anything and when I feel like I'm about to faint I eat a cube of cheese. I'm just one stomach flu away from my goal weight.*

Well it was Andy not Emily who somehow manages to make her way to Paris with Miranda, although Andy wins the trip to Paris and Miranda's admiration, she really looses because there is no victory in an empty victory. In Paris she see Miranda performs the ultimate betrayal towards her long time friend, her loyal fashion director Nigel, who also happens to be Andy's mentor. In attempts to save her own job, Miranda recommends Jacqueline Follet for a position that Nigel has had long coming. This is a wake up call for Andy she realizes that if she doesn't change she'll end up completely alone without friends; without a boyfriend, and worst of all without her self-respect. She sees that it is in her to become as cunning and cold as Miranda Presley. It is at this moment that she wonders if it's any good to have so much power and to be completely alone, empty and miserable. It is then that Andy truly finds her "whatever" and chooses not to become Miranda Presley. Like Andy, many of us have encountered these crossroads in our lives where the decision we make will affect the rest of our life for good or for bad, even more that that sometimes those decisions will affect our destiny beyond even our physical life. Destiny is one of the principles of Buddhism, to a certain degree it is a universal principle. I think that the notion that what we do now goes beyond our immediate realm and that it has series of effects and outcomes that will result because of our actions is the string that keeps us humans in line. Like Andy we all make mistakes but it is the ability to recognize our mistakes and to attempt to makes amends that leads to enlightenment.

Once Andy realized that she was living someone else's dream, she gets to see Miranda in the proper light and recognizes how utterly unhappy she is and that no amount of power or money will ever make her happy. That's Andy wake up call! Andy finds here whatever and begins to find her way back from the dark path she was headed on. I believe this is the beauty to life that no matter how badly any one of us manages to mess things up there is always a chance to make things right, if we choose to. Once Andy found her way back to normal things weren't exactly the same as in our lives things usually never end up the same once we have opened our eyes; once we have hit the road and found our whatever; that's why to begin with because we want to find out what's out there and what's inside.

Interpretation:

Everyone one of us has had big dreams; most of us at some point have even set out to conquer them. But conquering our dreams can be a scary, so we often reach out to others to find courage and inspiration, however courage doesn't come from an outside source it comes from within. Andy took the long round about way to find out that *"Love and compassion are necessities, not luxuries. Without them humanity cannot survive"... Dalai Lama*

Sure Miranda had fame and power but she was completely alone and empty. The lesson here is that each one of us has to find a balance between accomplishing our ambitions and keeping our own core values in tact. Without our values we are nothing.

Your Personal Road to Whatever

In life we are dealt a hand of cards; that hand can be any combination imaginable. It can be a royal flush or a complete washout but the hand does not guarantee whether we will win or loss the game, because the game is made up of an entire series of elements and conditions like bluffing, calling bluffs or folding. In this life there are people that are meant to win because the have every type of charm, beauty and money, yet they fail because no matter how privileged a person may be, he or she still has to find his or her own path. No one can do that for you, it cannot be set out before you; because if it is then it is not your path but someone else's path that you've taken.

And just as there are the "winners" that don't win, there is also the extreme opposite in those individuals that have all odds against them yet they manage to become what they set out to become. My friend Lee Yung, once told me that in his culture; he's Korean, that a person's life can be predicted by their astrological birth date and that this plays an integral role in the upbringing of a child. There are those that are destined for greatness and those that are not and for the most part they are treated accordingly. However, he said that even if the stars smile on a person and predict that he or she should be blessed with riches and greatness, if that person lacks the courage to go after his or her fortune then the Gods get angry and take it all away. Buddhists understand that there are no guarantees in this life and that each of us has to find our own path to whatever it is that makes us happy. Likewise, no two paths are alike.

We can all find the courage and the path to become whatever we desire by following the lessons that Buddha left for us over 2,500 years ago. The answered are there for us in the eightfold path of love, kindness and compassion. To this his Holiness the Dalai Lama says *"the purpose of our lives is to be happy."* I hope that each and every one of you will find the courage and the light to set forth in search of our own road to "WHATEVER!"

References

Biblegateway.com < http://www.biblegateway.com/
   passage/?search=Philippians+4:8

Borg, Marcus and Kornfield, Jack; Jesus & Buddha; The
   parallel sayings (2002)

Dalai Lama of Tibet; My Land My People (1997)

Facts of Life American Sitcom theme song (1988)

Farrelly Robert and Farrelly Peter; Shallow Hal (2001)

Landaw, Jonathon; Buddhism for Dummies

Lawrence, Marc; Music and Lyrics (2007)

Lee, Spike; Do the right thing (1989)

Merriam- Webster's Dictionary; <http://www.merriam-
   webster.com/dictionary/whatever>

Yong, Lee [Conversation paraphrased] (Dec 2007)

Weiseberger, Lauren; The Devil Wears Prada (2006)

Wiseman, Roseland and Fay, Tina; Mean Girls (2004)